really rotten Rhymes

Gabriel Fitzmaurice

Really Rotten Rhymes

Illustrated by Stella Macdonald

MERCIER PRESS
WHAT YOU NEED TO READ

MERCIER PRESS
Douglas Village, Cork
www.mercierpress.ie

Trade enquiries to Columba Mercier Distribution,
55a Spruce Avenue, Stillorgan Industrial Park, Blackrock, Dublin

978 1 85635 544 5

10 9 8 7 6 5 4 3 2

Mercier Press receives financial assistance from
the Arts Council / An Chomhairle Ealaíon

Printed and bound by CPI Mackays of Chatham, Chatham, Kent

For Éanna, Ciara
and Naoise McGarrigle

CONTENTS

BUZZ WOZ ERE

Introduction

When I was a kid, we learned poetry (off by heart) in school. Much of it was difficult and dull – at least to this kid's mind it was. But what saved poetry for me were the nursery rhymes I had learned at home and the rhymes we learned on the street. I loved them – they were ours: kids' rhymes for kids. Our street rhymes were real, they were naughty, they were cool – the kind of rhymes you wouldn't repeat in front of your parents. We took great delight in the fact that we could share them secretly among ourselves.

These *Really Rotten Rhymes*, drawn from my experience as a child, a parent and a teacher, are, I hope, poems that will appeal to that ADULTS KEEP OUT place that is so special to a child. They will, I know, also touch the child's (even if it is the naughty child's) place in many adult hearts. Lewd, crude and rude or deliciously disgusting? They are both, I hope.

Enjoy!

Gabriel Fitzmaurice

A Messy Eater

Tom's a messy eater,
He messes up the place,
Gravy on the table,
Pandy on his face.

Tom's a messy eater,
He gobbles up his food,
He says that that's the only way
It does him any good.

Tom's a messy eater,
No matter how you scold
He's got no table manners.
It's not that he's being bold,

He's just a messy eater
And that's the way he'll be
Until he gets a girlfriend.
Then he'll change. You'll see.

A Cross Boy

I'm a cross boy. I can't help it.
I get into trouble each day –
In trouble at home, in trouble at school
For the things that I do and I say.

Then I thought of a plan to get better,
To keep me from trouble, and so
I opened my mam's holy water
And drank the whole lot in one go.

I drank all my mam's holy water
She'd brought in a bottle from Lourdes,
I drank all my mam's holy water
Hoping that I would get cured.

But no! I'm as crazy as ever,
My plan didn't work. Never could.
I thought I'd get better by magic
But it takes more than that to get good.

I'm a cross boy. I can't help it.
I get into trouble here still
But even cross boys can do better.
I can try to do better. I will.

A Pimple on your Backside

A pimple on your backside
Is sore and itchy too
And you shouldn't really scratch it
But you do.

A pimple on your backside
Is lumpy to the touch
But what can you do about it?
Not much.

A pimple on your backside
Is something you don't need
And if you try to burst it
'Twill bleed.

A pimple on your backside
Is something no one wants,
I'd a pimple on my backside
Once –
And once was enough.

Believe me.
OUCH!

An Apple for the Teacher

'Bring apples to eat', the teacher said,
But me, I'd rather mush
So I threw mine down the toilet
But the apple wouldn't flush.

It just kept bobbing like a ball
As the flush foamed all about,
So I put my hand in the toilet bowl
And took the apple out.

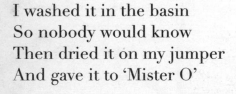

I washed it in the basin
So nobody would know
Then dried it on my jumper
And gave it to 'Mister O'

(That's what we call our teacher),
He rubbed it once or twice
And then he ate my apple.
He said 'twas very nice.

Belly Buttons

An 'inny' or an 'outie' –
A belly button goes
In like Dingle Harbour
Or out like the Pope's Nose.

An 'inny' or an 'outie' –
What kind of one have you?
I wish I had an 'inny'
'Cos mine sticks out. Boo hoo!

A Stinky Poem

This is a stinky poem
And, reading it, you'll find
The fumes that come out of this poem
Are only in your mind.

They're worse than dirty nappies,
They're worse than smelly socks,
They're worse than windy bottoms,
They're worse than lumpy snots.

They're worse, much worse, than slurry,
They're worse than a smelly loo,
They're worse than rotten rubbish,
They're worse than piggy's pooh.

They're worse, much worse than anything
You'll smell on land or foam
'Cos this smell is found nowhere.
Only in this poem.

21

A Walk in the Country

It's hard to find a toilet
When you're bursting for the loo
And you're somewhere in the country –
What are you to do?

You try to find a quiet spot
Behind a tree or ditch
But ouch! – ah yes, a nettle
Stings you and you itch.

And if, in desperation,
You sneak into a wood,
A crow is doing his business
And it lands upon your head.

Or if in haste you disappear
Down a shady lane,
Alas! The road less travelled
Ends up in a drain

And your socks and shoes are squelchy
And you wish you hadn't come
For a walk out in the country;
You turn around for home

'Cos it's hard to find a toilet
When you're bursting for the loo
And the countryside is treacherous
When you haven't got a clue.

MIDDLE OF
NOWHERE

23

At the Zoo

Last year on our school tour
We all went to the zoo,
We spent the whole day up there,
There was lots of things to do.

We saw camels there and crocodiles
And snakes and parrots too,
And bears, a hippopotamus
And a baby kangaroo.

We went into the monkey house –
We went in there with glee
'Cos we all love the monkeys
(They're great fun, you see);

I went over to the monkey cage
To have a closer look
When a monkey piddled in my eye –
Oh boy! What rotten luck.

The monkey just came over
And piddled in my eye
And I had nothing but my sleeve
To wipe it dry.

And I cursed that cheeky monkey
And I cursed that silly zoo
But my friends all started laughing
And I started laughing too
(What else could I do?).

Yes! I started laughing with them
But until the day I die
I won't forget the monkey
That piddled in my eye.

No! I won't forget the monkey
That piddled in my eye.

At the Seaside

When you paddle
In the sea
First you shiver
Then you pee
And the waves that licked your toes
Suddenly
Fizz up your nose
And you stumble
Oh the shock
And you swallow water
Yock
But it's sweaty summer weather
And it's great fun altogether

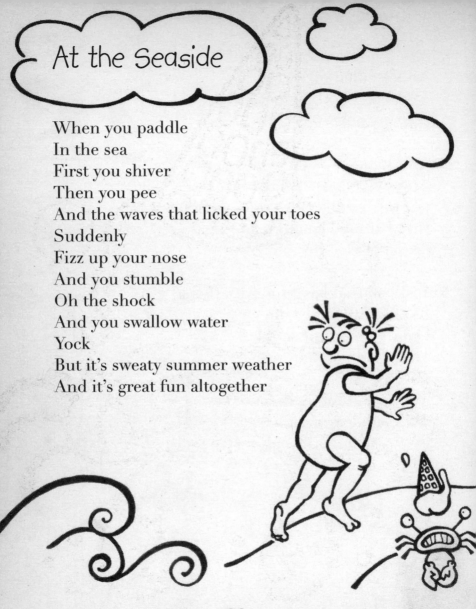

Aunt Jane

My Aunt Jane
Had dirty toes,
Dirty nails
And dirty clothes
And, when the wash-up
Time would come,
She'd wipe the knives
Across her bum.

And though you'd think
That doing that
Would make her sick,
Well, it did not –
She had resistance
To all dirt
That no bug
Could ever hurt.

Never sick
And never down,
She'd sing where other
Folks would frown;
She sang her troubles
Clean away.
They don't make folks
Like her today.

Aunt Jane.

Bursting Pimples

Did you ever burst a pimple?
It doesn't hurt at all –
The white stuff shoots right out of it
To the mirror on the wall;

And then you get a tissue
To mop up bits of blood
And you flush it down the toilet
And it goes off with the flood.

And you polish up the mirror
To get rid of all the goo
And you flush that down the toilet
Too.

Oh I love bursting pimples!
It doesn't hurt at all
When all the bad inside you
Is splattered on the wall.

'Bottom'

Why is it, hearing 'bottom'
You always seem to laugh?
What is it about 'bottom'
Makes everyone go daft?

You don't laugh at 'hand' or 'head'
Or 'leg' or 'nose' or 'toe'
Or 'hair' or 'eye' or 'nose' or 'wrist'
But at 'bottom' you go

Giggle-giggle-giggle,
There's nothing you can do
But laugh when you hear 'bottom'
For 'bottom' is the cue,

The password to your naughty mind
That you keep out of sight
And 'bottom' is really naughty
Although the word's polite.

Yes! 'bottom' is really naughty,
No matter what you do
To make it sound all nice and neat
It's the part that makes the pooh.

Your bottom!

Checkin' my Wellies for Spiders

I'm checkin' my wellies for spiders,
I turn them upside down,
I'm checkin' my wellies for spiders
Before I put them on.

I'm checkin' my wellies for spiders
'Cos they might be inside –
I know if I was a spider
'Twould be a brilliant hide.

I'm checkin' my wellies for spiders,
Once I had no fear
Of creepy things like spiders
But now I just can't bear

The thought of touchin' crawlies –
They give me the creeps
So I'm checkin' my wellies for spiders
Before I put in my feet.
Yeah! I'm checkin' my wellies for spiders
Before I put in my feet.

Do Teachers Fart?

Do teachers fart?
What do you think?
I stood beside one,
Smelled the stink.

But I don't think
A teacher would –
Aren't teachers always
Very good?

Do teachers fart?
I just can't tell
But if teacher didn't
Who made the smell?

Who?

Diarrhoea

I had a queasy tummy,
I went up to the loo
And when I'd done my business
I made pooh juice instead of pooh.

And that's true.

Did You ever eat a Worm?

Did you ever eat a worm?
Well, Willie used to do –
He'd get a great big lump of earth
And he'd eat that too.

And the more he chewed it
And the more the worm went in,
The more the earth and worm-guts
Went gooing down his chin.

Did you ever eat a worm?
Well, Willie often did
And, well, maybe you did too
When you were a kid

'Cos kids love earth and worms,
I don't know why they do
But they seem to get a kick
Out of guts and grime and goo.

They do!

Dreamy Thomas

Dreamy Thomas picks his nose –
He may not know it but he does,
Dreaming things that only he
In his wonderland can see.
He sticks his finger up his snout,
Turns his finger round about,
Turns it this way, turns it that,
Fills his nose up very fat
And when he takes it out again
His nose goes back to being thin.
And all the while he's dreaming dreams
Where nothing is as nothing seems,
Dreaming poems in a world of prose
While Dreamy Thomas picks his nose.

Dreamy Thomas.

He blows his Nose in the Tea-towel

He blows his nose in the tea-towel
And then he dries the ware,
I think it's disgusting
But Batty doesn't care.

He blows his nose in the tea-towel
But a tissue it is not,
He blows his nose in the tea-towel
And dries the ware with snots.

YUCK!

He sings when he's on the Toilet

He sings when he's on the toilet
(He talks to himself as well),
He thinks there's no one listening
And we all have to quell

Our giggles at his antics
While he's sitting on the throne,
Somehow, when you're in there,
You think you're all alone

And so you start up singing
And making speeches too
'Cos you think no one can hear you
When you're sitting on the loo.
Oh, you think no one can hear you
When you're sitting on the loo.

But they can!

Her first Flight

'I love you, Dad! I love you!
I love this massive plane –
It looks like a big fat pencil-case
(Aer Spain- is it, Dad? Aer Spain?).

'This aeroplane's exciting,
It's noise-ing up to go –
Will it drive as fast as you, Dad?
But, Dad, we're going slow'.

'We're driving to our runway, dear,
And then we'll go real fast –
Faster than even I drive'.
'Whee, Dad! Whee! At last!

'We're going really speedy,
When are we going to fly?
Wow! Up, up, up we go, Dad!
'Way up in the sky.

'What's happening to my ears, Dad?
They're funny – I can't hear
(Well, kind of); what you say, Dad?
There's something in my ears'.

'Suck a sweet, 'twill help you –
It's a good idea'.
'Who's Eddie, Dad? Eddie?'.
'I said it's a good *idea*.

'Look at the clouds now, Nessa,
We're coming to them – just;
In a minute we'll be through them'.
'Dad, it's like they're made of dust –

'The clouds are awful dusty,
I can't see a thing –
Just dark outside my window.
Now what's happening?

'We're above the clouds! The sunshine!'
'Sit back now and relax.
It's three hours to Tenerife –
Let's have a little nap'.

'Daddy, we're not moving –
Look down at the sea:
It's not moving, we're not moving;
This is boring – I have my wee.

'Daddy, where's the toilet?
I'm bored with this oul' plane'.
'Look out the window, Nessa –
Look down and you'll see Spain'.

'Daddy, where's the toilet?
Is there any on this plane?'
'OK, OK, I'll take you';
'Daddy, we're over Spain …

46

When I was at the toilet,
I made poops as well as wee –
'Where did the poops go, Daddy?
The poops I made, the wee?

'Did they fall down on some Spanish man
'Way 'way down below?
Where did my poops go, Daddy?
Where did my wee-wee go?

'What's next after Spain, Dad?
Will we get our dinner soon?
This aeroplane's exciting.
How far up is the moon?

'Dad, my ears are popping –
Is everything all right?
Daddy, oops! I chewed my sweet
I got such an awful fright.

'But it's OK now, Daddy –
It's just the plane going down.
Daddy, Daddy! Tenner Reef!
Dad, is this our town?'

TENERIFE

How Noreen got Stuck in her Knickers

She went for a sit on the toilet
And, however her bottom was placed,
Her bracelet got stuck in her knickers
And she couldn't get free. The disgrace!

They were state-of-the-art frilly knickers,
The bracelet was dripping with charms
And the charms got stuck in her knickers
And she had to raise the alarm.

And her uncle came into the toilet
And freed her with one little twist;
Now Noreen takes care with her knickers
When she's dripping with charms from her wrist.
She does.

When she's dripping with charms from her wrist.

How High?

How high can I piddle?
Higher than the door?
But the piddle hit it halfways up
And dribbled on the floor.

I got a ball of tissue
And rubbed the door till dry
And soaked it off the lino.
Wow! I can piddle high!

I'd Like to Be

I'd like to be a fat green snot
Snailing down your lip –
A silken, soupy, slimy snot
Dribble, dribble, drip!

You'd squelch me in through your front teeth,
Roll me 'round a bit
Then suck me back to shoot me out,
A swirling, swollen spit.

I Swallowed my Tooth when I was Young

I swallowed my tooth when I was young
But it worked out OK
(The tooth fairy came
Anyway).

I swallowed my tooth when I was young,
It was loose inside my mouth
And when it fell out of my gum
It went in instead of out.

I swallowed my tooth when I was young
But I didn't mind
'Cos my tooth went wiggling down my guts
And came out my behind.

I swallowed my tooth when I was young
And a permanent tooth appeared
Now I'm beyond that baby stuff
'Cos that was, well ... last year.

Jacko

Jacko is our cockatiel,
Jacko eats his pooh,
Mammy laughs at Jack and says
'That's men for you!'

Johnny Manners

Johnny Manners
Is a square
Tidy clothes
And tidy hair
Never plays
Or acts the mick
Johnny Manners
Makes me sick

'I Forgot'

He should have shared his sweets with Shane
But he ate the lot
And when his mammy asked him why,
He answered 'I forgot'.

He went out with his jumper on
When the sun was shining hot
And when his mammy asked him why,
He answered 'I forgot'.

He didn't use a tissue,
Instead he sucked his snot
And when his mammy asked him why,
He answered 'I forgot'.

 ME

He made his wee-wees in his pants
When he should have used the pot
And when his mammy asked him why,
He answered 'I forgot'.

He sat upon the toilet,
He didn't wipe his bot
And when his mammy asked him why,
He answered 'I forgot'.

He really doesn't mean to,
The poor guy's just a tot
Who, when his mammy asks him why,
Answers 'I forgot'.

He really doesn't mean to,
The poor guy's just a tot
Who, when his mammy asks him why,
Answers 'I forgot'.

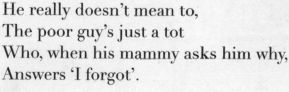

Johnny's False Teeth

Johnny fiddles with his teeth
While they're in his mouth –
He pops them up, he pops them down,
He pops them in and out.

He doesn't know he's doing it
(I think they need adjusting)
But he should keep them in his mouth
Because they look disgusting.

Infant

He spins around the floor.
When teacher tells him stop,
He stops, then spins a little more,
A human spinning top.

And when he's finished spinning,
He crawls, a little pup;
He stops, then crawls a little more
When teacher says 'Get up!'

And when we're sitting on our chairs,
Is he sitting? No! He kneels
And you can see his underpants
When he's sitting on his heels.

He's just a little infant
All scribble, dribble, thumb
Who pops his fingers in his mouth
When he's scratched his bum;

He's just a little infant
Barely turned four
Who crawls, a little puppy
And spins around the floor.

61

Mikey Spuds

Mikey Spuds is hairy
And Mikey Spuds is fat –
If he sat upon you
He'd squash you flat.

He has a pandy belly,
He stuffs it like a sow,
His belly's so enormous
He has no sideways now.

His pants is like a circus tent
It's so big and tall,
He always has to pull it up
For fear that it would fall.

His belly hangs out over it,
It hangs out by a mile
And when he bends to tie his lace
You can see his builder's smile

Beaming from his backside,
Winking up at you,
His backside's awful hairy
Too

'Cos Mikey Spuds is hairy
And Mikey Spuds is fat.
He's fatter than an elephant
And that's that.

Kissing on the Telly

Kissing on the telly
Makes me really sick,
Every time I see it
I get the remote and flick

To some other channel,
To football, racing, darts,
Kissing's just for sillies
Who draw these pink love hearts

On every bit of paper
That they come across,
I'd ban kissing if I could
And 'twould be no loss

'Cos kissing's really stupid,
It makes me want to puke.
If there's kissing on the telly
DON'T LOOK!

Love your Bum

'Love your bum', the slogan said.
Ugh! The thought of it –
An ad for toilet paper, I thought
This is pushing things a bit.

But then I got to thinking
It's good; no matter what,
Love is good for everything,
Even for your bot.

So love your bum. Believe me,
If you love like that, you'll find
That you can love most anything.
Even your behind.

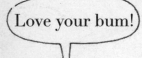

Love your bum!

Mussel

Is a mussel a male or a female?
It's a question that puzzles me so;
Is a mussel a male or a female?
And please someone, how would you know?

Is a mussel a male or a female?
And what would you look for? – you know,
Has it bits like the bits that we cover
(That make us female or male) with our clothes?

Is a mussel a male or a female?
Does it think? Does it feel? (Can you tell?);
Is a mussel a male or a female
Or a nothing inside in its shell?

Someone please
HELP!

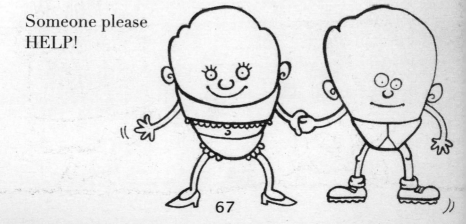

My new blue Knickers

I got new blue knickers
In a packet on a hook;
I'm wearing my new knickers –
Do you want to see them? LOOK!

I love my new blue knickers,
I'm proud as proud can be –
I can't wait to show my knickers.
EVERYBODY LOOK AT ME!

I got new blue knickers,
I'm proud as proud can be –
I'm ready, are you looking?
MY NEW BLUE KNICKERS – SEE!

My Yoghurt spilled in my Bag

My yoghurt spilled in my bag,
It stuck like snots to a rag
And no one would help,
I'd to clean it myself,
Now my books are so soggy they sag.

Onion Eater

I like to eat an onion
When I have a little drink –
I munch it like an apple
And BOY does my breath stink!

Number Two

When you're going to the toilet
And you make your number two
(Perhaps I should explain here –
That's what I call pooh),

And no matter how you flush it
You can't sink it like a boat
(Sometimes it's unsinkable,
A pooh that's meant to float),

And it sits there on the water
Daring you to try
Till you cover it with papers
And hope no one will spy

You as you sneak out
Defeated by the pooh,
You pray no-one will notice
This turd was made by you.

You do!

Piddling Song

I don't need a nappy
'Cos now I'm nearly three –
I tinkle in my potty.
Come here and watch me … See?

Pooh

Does pooh always come from your bottom?
Mammy, I need to find out.
I hope it just comes from your bottom.
I'd hate if it came from my mouth.

Porridge

It looks like puke or diarrhoea
But it's very good for me.

I like porridge.

Snots

Snots are gooey
Snots are sweet
Snots are chewy
Things to eat

Shampoo

When I sit in the hot water,
I make wee-wees in the bath
And no-one knows I've done it
But I don't worry about that.

And it's great to play with soap suds
And do splashy-splashy there
And you forget you've made your wee-wees
Till it's time to wash your hair.

And Daddy gets the shampoo
And it's too late to cry
That there's wee-wees in the water –
It's in your ears and eyes,

It's running down your nose and mouth,
There's nothing you can do,
And Daddy says you've nice clean hair
When he's finished the shampoo.

Something attempted, Something done

This little boy in Infants
Can't wipe his bot
So he comes in to his teacher
(God bless the little tot)

With his trousers 'round his ankles
And says 'Please, Miss, will you
Wipe my botty-wotty
Because I made a pooh'.

So she takes him to the toilet
And shows him what to do
Now he can wipe his botty-wot
When he's in the loo.

Good man yourself!

The Champion

Paddy's a champion burper,
He burps with all of his might,
He burped such a whopper this morning
He tasted his supper last night.

For Paddy's a champion burper,
He burps like no other kid can
And you'd swear from the tone and the volume
His burps were made by a man.
The Champion!

Puke

Puke is stinky,
Puke is thick,
The smell of puke
Would make you sick.

Puke is lumpy,
Looks like soup
But you couldn't drink
A bowl of puke

'Cos puke comes up
And soup goes down
And both are lumpy,
Thick and brown;

Yes! Both are lumpy,
Brown and thick
But soup is nice
And puke is sick.

YUCK!

Spider

Hairy spider on the wall!
John stiffens, John bawls;

Cool as you like while John fretted,
Nessa picked it up and ate it.

Sunburn

When you're lying in the sun
Your skin gets burned; you treat it;
And then when it begins to peel
You pick it off and eat it.

Snotty Tanner

Snotty Tanner
Licks his snots,
The snots run down
His lip a lot.

He tries to suck 'em
Up his nose
But the more he sucks
The more they go

Snailing slimy
Down his lip,
He has to lick 'em
Or they'll drip;

He has to lick 'em
Look! Like this!
And no one asks him
For a kiss

For if he kissed you
With his snots,
Would you like it?
You would not;

You wouldn't like
A kiss like that,
A snotty kiss
All green and fat.

NO WAY!

Strimming the Garden

Did you ever swallow pooh?
Well Daddy did.
It's true.

He was strimming the front garden,
He was singing a little song,
Singing a song to cheer himself
As he strimmed along.

Well anyway
He didn't see
The dog's pooh
When, gracious me!
The strimmer shot the pooh
Into Daddy's mouth

And Daddy had it swallowed
Before he could spit it out.

He gargled, gargled, gargled –
Well, that's all you can do
(But it makes no difference)
When you swallow pooh.

He gargled, gargled, gargled
And the next time he went out
Strimming the front garden
Was Daddy singing?

No way!

He shut his mouth.

The Parcel

My name for it was 'parcel'
(Pooh-poohs in my pants),
And when you had to walk with it,
You made a kind of dance

With a wiggle and a waggle
And a sideways kind of glance
Going home to Mammy
With a parcel in your pants.

And all the village noticed
By the funny way you'd walk,
And you had to brave the gauntlet
Of the whistles, squeals and squawks;

And even your friends would tease you,
Hold their noses, cry 'the stink!'
Till you got home to Mammy
And she'd wash you at the sink.

And she'd put you in new trousers
And advise you once again
To be sure and use the toilet
Before you went out with your friends.

The true story
of Little Miss Muffet

Little Miss Muffet
Sat on a spider
(He couldn't get away) –
He went SPLAT!
She squashed him flat
And his guts came out like whey.

SPLAT!

It didn't come from outer space
(If it did, I wouldn't care) –
Oh no! it was much worse than that
When a bird pooped on my hair.

I was minding my own business
Playing in the yard
When I felt this plop upon my head
Catching me off guard.

When I reached up to investigate,
I felt this sticky goo
And all my friends were laughing
That my hair was stuck with pooh.

90

And then I started crying –
I cried most bitterly
That of all the places that pooh could land
It had to land on me.

And I wouldn't let them wash me –
Oh Lord! It wasn't fair
So I just sat and sulked and sobbed
That a bird pooped on my hair.

I just sat and sulked and sobbed
That a bird pooped on my hair.

The First Christmas

Was there a smell from the cow in the stable?
Did the ass rise his tail up and bray?
Was there animals' poops 'round the manger
In Bethlehem that Christmas Day?

Did the sheep keep quiet for the shepherds?
Was the baby able to play?
Did his mother croon when she burped him
In Bethlehem that Christmas Day?

Did Joseph know how to change nappies?
And the angels – did they fly away?
If I was about, I'd have sussed all that out
In Bethlehem that Christmas Day.

The Kangaroo

He's just a little Infant
And when he went to use the loo,
He pulled his trousers to his heels
To make a pooh.

But the loo was out of order
And before he made his pooh,
He hopped out of the toilet
Like a kangaroo,

His trousers 'round his ankles,
Hopping so he could
Get to another toilet;
You can't walk very good

With your trousers 'round your ankles
So he hopped across the floor,
Out of the toilet, through the hall,
Down the corridor,

And when the girls saw him,
They gave him such a dusting –
They turned away and, in one voice,
Said 'JOHNNY YOU'RE DISGUSTING!'

When you make a Smelly

When you make a smelly,
What are you to do?
You act like all the others
And pretend it wasn't you.

When you make a smelly,
You hide it, so you do,
And hope no one will notice
The smelly came from you.

You do!